D1563321

PIERRE ÉCRITE | WORDS IN STONE

UNIVERSITY OF MASSACHUSETTS PRESS   AMHERST   1976

PIERRE ÉCRITE | WORDS IN STONE

Yves Bonnefoy   Translated by Susanna Lang

English text and translator's note
Copyright © 1976 by Susanna Lang
Introduction and bibliography
Copyright © 1976 by The University of Massachusetts Press
French text copyright © by Mercure de France
All rights reserved
Library of Congress Catalog Card Number 75-32481
ISBN 0-87023-203-7
Reproductions of Ubac lithographs courtesy of
Galerie Maeght

Printed in the United States of America

Library of Congress Cataloging in Publication Data
Bonnefoy, Yves
Words in stone = Pierre écrite.
Bibliography: p.
I. Lang, Susanna, 1956–   II. Title.   III. Title:
Pierre écrite.
PQ2603.0533P513   841'.9'14   75-32481
ISBN 0-87023-203-7

For Mortimer Guiney,
who introduced me to the poet
and to the poetry.
S.A.L.

CONTENTS

WORDS IN STONE

A FIRE GOES BEFORE US

THE DIALOGUE BETWEEN ANGUISH AND DESIRE

Introduction

Yves Bonnefoy is one of the major poets to come into prominence in France after World War II, and is probably the major French lyric poet of this period. He writes a metaphysical poetry of modern times, whose clear, depersonalized voice gives aesthetic form to questions of being and nothingness, identity and communion, speech and silence—the ways of consciousness.

The Heideggerian themes of Bonnefoy's poetry are familiar to a general audience as part of existential literature in the post-war period, especially in the novels and plays of Sartre and Camus. As an existential poet, however, Bonnefoy does not seem influenced by his contemporaries so much as by earlier art and literature. Gothic murals, Piero della Francesca, Bernini and Rubens, Racine, Baudelaire, the Gnostics and Hegel, all exist in the background of Bonnefoy's poems. His style combines the allusive imagery, precision, and density of Symbolist poetry with the Surrealist's visionary self-consciousness and leaps of the imagination. The work of this first existentialist poet, as St. Aubyn has called him, is secured in a continuing aesthetic and philosophical tradition.

Bonnefoy was born on June 24, 1923, in Tours, the capital of Touraine and a city whose importance in French history dates back to the fourth century. He studied mathematics at Tours and at Poitiers, and then went to Paris to continue studies in philosophy. From 1945 to 1947, he was associated with the Surrealist group and read Chestov and Kierkegaard. Later he did research in art history and prepared a thesis on English and American criticism, and on Piero della Francesca. Bonnefoy received a *licence ès lettres* and a *diplôme d'études supérieures de philosophie*, and his essays on art and literature reveal this broad training at the same time that they reflect the poet's own themes.

Although Bonnefoy is best known as a poet, he has translated a number of Shakespearean plays (*The Winter's Tale, Julius Caesar, Hamlet, King Lear, Romeo and Juliet*), written several books of art history, and been editor of *L'Ephémère*, a journal of contemporary art and poetry, from 1966 to 1973. A frequent lecturer in American universities for many years, his professional connection with the French university system began with an appointment to Vincennes in 1969. He was associated with the University of Nice from 1973 to 1976, and divided his time between Nice and Paris. As a poet, translator, editor and essayist, Bonnefoy pursues a single meditation on art and existence: on the way art intuits and expresses, in calculated yet imperfect language, the complex self-awareness of our human condition.

Bonnefoy writes difficult poetry in simple language. Individual images and scenes are beautiful in themselves, individual statements appear simple and clear; yet the total effect is often paradoxical, or tantalizingly open-ended. *Simplicity* is a word that recurs often in Bonnefoy's work, and it implies not superficiality but a basic rightness, a correspondence with *things as they are*. To achieve this simplicity, the poet must lead his readers into a closed, almost hermetic poetic world where each reality is completed by its opposite. Presence and absence, life and death, perfection and a fuller imperfection, concrete and abstract, are all so many levels of a total reality which the poet must reveal. The most difficult opposition to grasp is that of life and death, and it remains central to Bonnefoy's argument from the Hegelian epigraph to *Douve* ("Now the life of the spirit does not cringe before death, nor keep itself pure from it. It supports death and maintains itself in it") to the line from Shakespeare's *Winter's Tale* opening *Pierre écrite:* "Thou mettest with things dying: I with things newborn." The simplicity of full vision is achieved only after a complex, difficult search for true understanding.

Christian metaphors play a great part in this poetry, although they do not indicate any hope of otherworldly salvation. Rather, Bonnefoy transposes the themes and images of Christian idealism to convey the burning wish for transcendence that pervades his purely humanistic philosophy. The ship and journey metaphors of *Words in Stone* (*Pierre écrite*), the ambiguous flow and metamorphosis of *On the Motion and Immobility of Douve* (*Du mouvement et de l'immobilité de Douve*), the passage between two shores of the underworld in *In the Illusion of the Threshold* (*Dans le leurre du seuil*) are all aspects of a central quest that leads to an earthly Grail. In modern French poetry, says Bonnefoy, there is a "procession of the Grail which passes, the most alive things of this earth—tree, face, stone—and they must be named." Bonnefoy turns the sense of the Grail legend in upon itself: where Parsifal was not bold enough to question the Grail carried before him, the poet will name what he sees; where Joseph of Arimathea's earthen cup was transmuted by the blood of Christ into a mystical chalice, Bonnefoy's Grail becomes an earthen vessel and vision of immanence.

In *Words in Stone*, Bonnefoy's quest for the Grail begins with an intuition of the return to Eden, and it is completed by encounters with death and materiality as elements that must be incorporated into a final vision. The voice of God does not appear through a burning bush, but the bush itself becomes a sign of the angel. "The angel, who is the earth, /

Enters each bush, to appear there and burn. / I am the empty altar . . ." Communion on this empty altar and from this earthen cup does not invoke the presence of transcendent divinity. It symbolizes a relationship between human consciousness and what is outside; the typical existential awareness of Self and Other, clothed here in religious symbols. This otherness may be material: the hard surface of stone in which an artist inscribes traces of human will and desire, or it may be the stony grayness of words, in which the writer plunges the "red blade" of his experience. Bonnefoy is impelled to see himself in relation to the otherness outside his own human consciousness, and he adds aesthetic force to this philosophical impulse by comparing it with the mystical desire for another world. His poetry makes frequent references to an "other" day, an "other" summer, or an "other" world, using the imagery of traditional religious idealism to imply a fuller vision of this same earth. In naming the things of this earth, says Bonnefoy, modern poetry names its own procession of the Grail: establishes its own search for the equally elusive Grail of total understanding.

The quest for an earthen Grail leads Bonnefoy to see this world as a "true place," a "here and now" that must be recognized for itself and not as the threshold of things to come. Images of "place" and "threshold" reappear frequently in this poetry, and always with the feeling that the wished-for Eden is not just across the threshold, but is the threshold itself from which we intuit a possible transcendence.

Bonnefoy's task is to describe this "here and now" in "essentialized" terms that will let us grasp the abstract in the concrete. The blending of real and ideal occurs in a spare, almost mythological description which avoids long descriptive passages, chooses essentialized words, and works within the framework of a consciously limited vocabulary. Bonnefoy is quite specific in "The Act and Place of Poetry" about how he chooses essentialized rather than particularized words: "stone," for example, rather than "brick." Essentialized language is not an escape from reality into abstract idealism: Bonnefoy retains specific concrete details like the "foam at Trieste" to pin the poem down to a particular place on earth. However, his poetry aims at an impression of mythological clarity and precision by stripping the language bare of extended particularized description. Richness is obtained by the shifting of voice and of perspective inside a same horizon. Red is almost the only color used, and there is a characteristic landscape composed of a few essential elements: flat surfaces, light and darkness, foliage and germination, water, stone, and earth. Relationships change inside this landscape: the ship is earth, summer, or life; sky is an angel's shoulder; time "lies in pools of color." Mythological references join with Christian images to interpret the appearance of reality: the phoenix dies and rises from its ashes, and the salamander lives in its bed of flames. Angles of vision are displaced and different, and unnamed voices speak to one another and to the writer. Inside a picture composed of a limited number of the most ordinary words, Bonnefoy employs unexpected associations, symbolic structures, and existential themes to let us see a complexly interwoven "beyond" immanent in the framework of everyday experience.

Art alone makes us aware of this complex experience. The grief of Tintoretto's Pieta, says Bonnefoy, is a cause of spiritual awakening because of its aesthetic "elegance." Emotion tears through the veil of the painted image, but only because of the image can that emotion appear. In the last poem of *Words in Stone*, "Art of Poetry," Bonnefoy attributes to poetry the power of regeneration that creates a new Eden. Here, the poet's "look" or power to see has been dredged up from the depths of night, and a "bloody, disconsolate voice" has been "washed and called forth" to live again.

This resurrection of an artistic voice is not a secure and comfortable promise of immortality, the kind of doctrinaire salvation that Verlaine achieved towards the end of his career. Resurrection in Bonnefoy is an imperfect salvation, an imperfection that he has already called a "summit" above perfection itself. Any ideal of eternal, unchanging perfection is unacceptable to a poet of the *here and now*, who celebrates his perpetual awareness of an unfinished, unstable reality. Bonnefoy's poet must accept his own disappearance, yet find a way to describe it. He composes the poetry of being and nothingness in an unfinished "dialogue between anguish and desire"—between the desire for transcendence, and the anguished awareness of earth. The words in stone symbolize this harsh partnership between human will and inert materiality. Their inscribed stone marks the poet's decision to celebrate the existential consciousness in its earthly paradise.

Sarah Lawall

Translator's Note

When I first read Bonnefoy's work, its coherence over-
whelmed me; and this quality has continued to be of pri-
mary importance in translating the book. The poems do
not repeat, one after another, the first poem in the book;
but every poem is so intimately connected to every other
that the entire book is implicit in each. A single poem is
often one of a series, such as that which begins *Pierre
Écrite*: the series is, in turn, part of a section; the section,
one of several in the book; and the book, a continuation
of the earlier books and a prelude to the next. In each,
questions raised many times before are extended, phrased
with more precision, and occasionally answered in a burst
of energy and light.

As the individual poems are interrelated, so are the dif-
ferent levels within the poems. Their purpose, their voice,
and their shape on the page are all accessible once the
work is understood in any of its aspects. For example,
Bonnefoy takes a particular interest in the look of his
books. Because he has shaped the visual medium, so often
dormant in poetry, to reinforce the imagistic and meta-
physical sense of the book, his concern is not limited to
the worries shared by all poets: that the poems be legible,
that lines not be divided, etc. The first, and partial, edition
of *Pierre Écrite* was published in 1958, accompanied by
Raoul Ubac's lithographs, one of which forms the cover of
this edition. "*Pierre écrite*" is quite literally the ancient art
of inscription, of words carved in stone, but it may also be
lithography, images in stone. Thus many of the poems in
the present collection are titled "*Une Pierre*" ("A Stone")
and are centered on the page, rather than being attached to

the left margin. The white page becomes the stone itself, and the words are slowly and painfully set in place, a texture as well as a visual design. A single voice, the stone's voice or the sculptor's, unifies these poems: and by "voice" I mean both the words themselves, enduring record of a voice that once spoke, and the tone of voice which is not the words but the sensibility which chose the words. The ultimate goal for these poems may be imaged as the threshold of another world, from which the unchanging, otherworldly voice of this world's stones is clearly heard; this image is identical to our retinal image of the poem on the page, shaped like writing on a headstone; and it is further the same as the voice we hear when we read the poems aloud, the poet speaking in the *persona* of a stone.

This much may be understood simply by reading the text; but it is interesting to know that Bonnefoy's point of departure was an actual place in southern France, the Défilé de Pierre Écrite. Towards the end of the Empire, Roman civilization had retreated before the advancing barbarians. In an inaccessible stronghold, the Romans maintained, for a while, their culture, leaving behind them an inscription in stone, testifying to their effort. For Bonnefoy, they had borne witness to the human condition: before the word there was neither being nor nothingness; the word carved in stone converts matter itself to meaning, and wards off the encroaching darkness.

A network of images comprehensive enough to express an entire ontology creates a problem for Bonnefoy's translator. If the reader is to make the necessary connections between the terms which define Bonnefoy's system, these terms must be as consistent in the translation as in the original. It is not sufficient to solve a problem as it relates to one poem; the solution must apply throughout the book.

The key terms are chosen from a limited vocabulary,

which compounds the difficulty. Beneath the intellectual splendor and the smooth surface of the poems, a few, trustworthy words expose the poet's essential vulnerability. He hopes and believes that *l'être*, Ultimate Being, is to be found at the center of material things—the voice from the stones, a transparency at the core of density, a sort of eternity. He does not conceive of the eternal as a cure for death, but rather as an extreme sensitivity to the things of this world, a sensitivity so extreme that it can be a certainty. He forces himself, in an act of intense concentration, to see the essential within the stone, the tree, in any familiar object. The things we know are turned inside out, made unfamiliar, as their mysteries are shown to us, but without limiting the mystery by defining it, and without lessening the original vision. The images which accomplish this feat are those which must be kept consistent; one hovers between the transcendent and the concrete while moving from French, with its purified vocabulary, to English and a wide vocabulary enriched by the contributions of multiple root languages. That is to say, it is easy in French to stress the abstract, otherwordly aspects of Bonnefoy's writing, while in English it is more natural to visualize a particular stone in a particular place. Because so many words are available to us in English, each has a specific referent and the distinctions between one word and another are very fine; whereas in French, a word carries a larger range of meanings, and may not necessarily be understood in such detail. It is easier, then, to maintain a consistent vocabulary in French, since words are more versatile. This difference between French and English is so well recognized, by Bonnefoy among others, that it is becoming a truism; but the consequences for the translator, and for the reader, are none the less real for being recognized.

The rhythms present similar problems: as with the vocabulary, Bonnefoy's technical choices are determined by his metaphysics and by his aesthetics, and it is impossible to distinguish between the different levels of choice. Much can be said, and has been very well said, about Bonnefoy's versification. It has been noted that he rejects what is arbitrary in the tradition of French verse, and that he is comfortable with extremely short lines as well as with traditional verse lines. His poems may give the impression of being rhymed, but the impression is created by the smoothness of the rhythms and by his careful use of sound patterns, not by terminal rhyme. As he has himself stated, he accepts those laws which are the very structure of the language and which extend the language, making it more flexible.[1] But many lines remain ambiguous: he has a special fondness for an eleven-syllable line which does not settle into the formality of the alexandrine or the more simple, narrative quality of the decasyllabic line.

Several of Bonnefoy's critics have commented on his open-ended versification, relating the length of his lines, his unpredictable use of the hiatus, etc., to his philosophy, as should be done. Jean-Pierre Richard in particular has said that Bonnefoy's slightly irregular lines fracture any formal perfection or concept-bounded Beauty in the poems, in order to introduce a harsher reality.[2] But there

1. I am endebted for much of my understanding of Bonnefoy's meters to F. Deloffre, "Versification traditionnelle et versification libérée d'après un recueil d'Yves Bonnefoy," *Le vers Français au 20e siècle: Colloqué organisé par le Centre de Philologie et de Littérature romanes de l'Université de Strasbourg du 3 mai au 6 mai 1966* (Paris: Klincksieck, 1967).
2. "Yves Bonnefoy," *Onze études sur la poésie moderne* (Paris: aux Éditions du Seuil, 1964), p. 231.

is more to it than may be analyzed with the usual tools of prosody. The rhythm is one thing, the metaphysics another, though they are indeed connected; then there is a certain tone of voice, which does not change as the voices change, and which announces Bonnefoy's poems as his own. Likewise, one can identify Bach's music with the first phrase, whether it is the opening of a harpsichord concerto or of an aria, whether the movement is slow or fast. Bonnefoy does, in fact, cherish Baroque architecture; and it is typical that he chooses to discuss the architecture, the expression of the Baorque in stone, rather than the music or the painting. Within the ornately decorated stone, there is a silence which overtakes the larger silence outside the walls; as, within Bonnefoy's own poems, there is a silence which is the imminence of another world and which is like that of the still moments in the day: dawn or evening, the settings for several of these poems. And this silence exists *through* the small noises which do not stop at any time in the day: the murmuring birds, the various sounds of the sea on the beach, the humming of bees. In the same way, the quiet at the center of Baroque art is the *reason for* the "loud" ornamentation.

Both the traditionalism and the originality of Bonnefoy's meters are peculiarly French and cannot be translated, as we have a different tradition with which to agree or differ. Yet this tone of voice, or this silence, must exist in the English or the translations have failed as poetry. It is peculiarly Bonnefoy's, as are the personal symbols and the limited vocabulary, and as the meter is peculiarly French. In addition, there is in the poetry an underpinning of Greek, Celtic and Gnostic myth which belongs to our history as much as to the French. When a whole society believed that to name a thing was to gain power over it, the poet was the only priest. More recently, the Romantic poet was again a prophet, in France, England and America. This faith in the power of the word is thus a familiar tradition. As a network of mythical allusions joins the more private aspects of Bonnefoy's work, in which he pays court to silence, a whole domain is created within the poetry which is more easily accessible to the English reader and to the translator. The public and private worlds cohere, as do the elements within each realm. Having entered Bonnefoy's world by way of an age-old tradition, we can understand the new conventions which he has created by analogy with what we have already understood; and I, as translator, may build an English poem on a foundation which is neither French nor English, neither mine nor Bonnefoy's alone.

Acknowledgements

Yves Bonnefoy's patience in answering my questions, and his willingness to discuss his intentions with me, have made the translation of this book a wonderfully exciting experience; and his approval is more than adequate payment for work I would have been glad to give. I am grateful, too, for the opportunity to benefit from Sarah Lawall's more profound intuition of Bonnefoy's work. George Pistorius, of Williams College, and Galway Kinnell, already a translator of Bonnefoy's poetry, as well as Mortimer Guiney, of the University of Connecticut, have all contributed excellent commentary and suggestions. Susan Parsons, also of Williams College, helped me to find the time to finish the translation.

S.A.L.

Thou mettest with things dying;
I with things new born.
The Winter's Tale

L'ÉTÉ DE NUIT | SUMMER OF NIGHT

L'ÉTÉ DE NUIT

I

Il me semble, ce soir,
Que le ciel étoilé, s'élargissant,
Se rapproche de nous; et que la nuit,
Derrière tant de feux, est moins obscure.

Et le feuillage aussi brille sous le feuillage,
Le vert, et l'orangé des fruits mûrs, s'est accru,
Lampe d'un ange proche; un battement
De lumière cachée prend l'arbre universel.

Il me semble, ce soir,
Que nous sommes entrés dans le jardin, dont l'ange
A refermé les portes sans retour.

I

This evening it seems to me
That the starlit sky grows larger
And draws near us; that behind so many fires
The night is less dark.

And the foliage burns beneath the foliage; the green
Swells, and the orange of the ripe fruit:
Lamp in the hand of a near-by angel;
A beating of hidden light overtakes the one tree.

This evening it seems to me
That we have entered that garden whose doors
The unreturning angel closed.

II

Navire d'un été,
Et toi comme à la proue, comme le temps s'achève,
Dépliant des étoffes peintes, parlant bas.

Dans ce rêve de mai,
L'éternité montait parmi les fruits de l'arbre
Et je t'offrais le fruit qui illimite l'arbre
Sans angoisse ni mort, d'un monde partagé.

Vaguent au loin les morts au désert de l'écume,
Il n'est plus de désert puisque tout est en nous
Et il n'est plus de mort puisque mes lèvres touchent
L'eau d'une ressemblance éparse sur la mer.

O suffisance de l'été, je t'avais pure
Comme l'eau qu'a changée l'étoile, comme un bruit
D'écume sous nos pas d'où la blancheur du sable
Remonte pour bénir nos corps inéclairés.

II

Ship of a summer,
And you as if at the prow, as time fails,
Unfolding painted cloths, talking softly.

In this May-dream
Eternity climbed among the tree's fruit
And I offered you the fruit which saves the tree
Without anguish or death, in a shared world.

Far off the dead wander in the desert surf;
There is no more desert since all is in us
And there is no more death since my lips touch
A mirror like water scattered on the sea.

The fullness of summer! For me, you were
Pure as the water the star changed, as the noise
Of the surf under our steps, where the white of the sand
Rises to bless our unclear bodies.

III

Le mouvement
Nous était apparu la faute, et nous allions
Dans l'immobilité comme sous le navire
Bouge et ne bouge pas le feuillage des morts.

Je te disais ma figure de proue
Heureuse, indifférente, qui conduit,
Les yeux à demi-clos, le navire de vivre
Et rêve comme il rêve, étant sa paix profonde,
Et s'arque sur l'étrave où bat l'antique amour.

Souriante, première, délavée,
A jamais le reflet d'une étoile immobile
Dans le geste mortel.
Aimée, dans le feuillage de la mer.

III

Movement
Seemed to us a sin, and we came
And went in immobility as under the ship
The foliage of the dead moves and does not move.

I called you my figurehead:
Halcyon, indifferent, who leads
With half-closed eyes the ship of living,
Who dreams as the ship dreams, who is its peace,
An arched back over the beat of antique love at the bow.

Smiling, primeval, sea-washed,
Forever the image of an unmoving star
In our mortal gestures.
Loved, in the foliage of the sea.

IV

Terre comme gréée,
Vois,
C'est ta figure de proue,
Tachée de rouge.

L'étoile, l'eau, le sommeil
Ont usé cette épaule nue
Qui a frémi puis se penche
A l'Orient où glace le coeur.

L'huile méditante a régné
Sur son corps aux ombres qui bougent,
Et pourtant elle ploie sa nuque
Comme on pèse l'âme des morts.

IV

Earth
Rigged like a ship, look:
Your figurehead,
Spotted with red.

The star, the sea, sleep
Have worn bare this shoulder
That trembled and now leans
Toward the East where hearts freeze.

The deep-thinking oil reigned
Over her body of moving shadows,
But still she bends her neck
As one weighs the soul of the dead.

V

Voici presque l'instant
Où il n'est plus de jour, plus de nuit, tant l'étoile
A grandi pour bénir ce corps brun, souriant,
Illimité, une eau qui sans chimère bouge.

Ces frêles mains terrestres dénoueront
Le noeud triste des rêves.
La clarté protégée reposera
Sur la table des eaux.

L'étoile aime l'écume, et brûlera
Dans cette robe grise.

V

Almost now
There is no more day, no night; the star
Has grown so large for the blessing of this brown body,
Smiling and boundless, a sea moving without deceit.

These frail hands of earth will
Untie this knot, our dreams.
Protected, the light will rest
On the plateau of the sea.

The star loves the surf, and will burn
In this grey robe.

. . . VI

Longtemps ce fut l'été. Une étoile immobile
Dominait les soleils tournants. L'été de nuit
Portait l'été de jour dans ses mains de lumière
Et nous nous parlions bas, en feuillage de nuit.

L'étoile indifférente; et l'étrave; et le clair
Chemin de l'une à l'autre en eaux et ciels tranquilles.
Tout ce que est bougeait comme un vaisseau qui tourne
Et glisse, et ne sait plus son âme dans la nuit.

... VI

That was the long summer. An unmoving star
Rose above the turning suns. The summer of night
Carried the summer of day in its hands of light
And we talked to each other softly, in the night foliage.

The indifferent star and the bowsprit; and the clear
Road from one to the other through seas and calm skies.
All that is, moved like a ship that turns
And glides, and does not know its own soul in the night.

VII

N'avions-nous pas l'été à franchir, comme un large
Océan immobile, et moi simple, couché
Sur les yeux et la bouche et l'âme de l'étrave,
Aimant l'été, buvant tes yeux sans souvenirs,

N'étais-je pas le rêve aux prunelles absentes
Qui prend et ne prend pas, et ne veut retenir
De ta couleur d'été qu'un bleu d'une autre pierre
Pour un été plus grand, où rien ne peut finir?

VII

Didn't we have the summer to cross, like a wide unmoving ocean,
And myself, simple, lying flat against
The eyes and the mouth and the soul of the bowsprit,
Loving the summer, drinking your forgetful eyes,

Wasn't I the dream with the absent eyes:
Taking, not taking, wanting to keep
Of your summer color only the blue of another stone
For a larger summer where nothing can end?

VIII

Mais ton épaule se déchire dans les arbres,
Ciel étoilé, et ta bouche recherche
Les fleuves respirants de la terre pour vivre
Parmi nous ta soucieuse et désirante nuit.

O notre image encor,
Tu portes près du coeur une même blessure,
Une même lumière où bouge un même fer.

Divise-toi, qui es l'absence et ses marées.
Accueille nous, qui avons goût de fruits qui tombent,
Mêle-nous sur tes plages vides dans l'écume
Avec les bois d'épave de la mort,

Arbre aux rameaux de nuit doubles, doubles toujours.

VIII

But the trees tear your shoulder, sky
Bright with stars, your mouth gropes in the earth
For a life among our breathing rivers;
We are your night, anxious and craving.

Our image still,
You carry the same wound close to your heart,
The same light, and quiver of iron.

You who are absence and its tides: divide yourself.
Gather us up, who taste like the fruits that fall;
On your strands bare in the surf
Blend us with the dead wood left by the sea;

You, whose limbs are the night, branched, and branched again.

IX

Eaux du dormeur, arbre d'absence, heures sans rives,
Dans votre éternité une nuit va finir.
Comment nommerons-nous cet autre jour, mon âme,
Ce plus bas rougeoiement mêlé de sable noir?

Dans les eaux du dormeur les lumières se troublent.
Un langage se fait, qui partage le clair
Buissonnement d'étoiles dans l'écume.
Et c'est presque l'éveil, déjà le souvenir.

IX

Sleeper's seas, tree of absence, shoreless hours
—In your eternity a night will end.
How will we name this other day, my soul,
This low-lying glow mixed with black sand?

Lights are muddied in the sleeper's seas.
Words emerge, divide the glowing
Foliage: stars in the surf.
—Almost awake, even a memory.

UNE PIERRE

«Regarde-moi
Là-bas, dans cet espace que transit
Une eau rapide et noire... »

Je t'inventais
Sous l'arche d'un miroir orageux, qui prenait
La parcelle d'un rouge en toi, impartageable,
Et l'enflammait «là-bas», au mascaret de mort.

A STONE

"Look for me down
There, in the river-mouth
Numbed by the rising of a sea, rapid and black . . ."

I invented you
Beneath the arch of a stormy mirror, which mimicked
A scrap of your red—inimitable—
And kindled the color "down there," on the surge of death.

LE JARDIN

Les étoiles voûtaient les murs du haut jardin
Comme les fruits de l'arbre au-delà, mais les pierres
Du lieu mortel portaient dans l'écume de l'arbre
Comme une ombre d'étrave et comme un souvenir.

Étoiles et vous, craies d'un pur chemin,
Vous pâlissiez, vous nous preniez le vrai jardin,
Tous les chemins du ciel étoilé faisant ombre
Sur ce chant naufragé; sur notre route obscure.

THE GARDEN

Stars arched over the walls of the high garden
Like fruit in the tree beyond, but stones from the mortal ground
Lay in the surf of the tree
Like the shadow of a bowsprit, or of a memory.

The stars and you, white stones on a pure road:
You paled, you seized the true garden;
All the roads in the starlit sky
Cast shadows on this shipwrecked song: our dark way.

Dans ses coffres le rêve a replié
Ses étoffes peintes, et l'ombre
De ce visage taché
De l'argile rouge des morts.

Tu n'as pas voulu retenir
Ces mains étroites qui firent
Le signe de solitude
Sur les pentes ocres d'un corps.

Et telle une eau qui se perd
Dans les rougeurs d'une eau sombre,
La nuque proche se courbe
Sur la plage où brille la mort.

Dream has folded its painted cloths
Into its coffers, along with the shadow
Of that face, stained
With the red clay of the dead.

You did not want
To hold back those narrow hands
That made the sign of solitude
Over the ochre slopes of a body.

Like water
Lost in the red of a darker water,
The head is bowed
Over the beach where death gleams.

L'ÉCUME, LE RÉCIF

Solitude à ne pas gravir, que de chemins!
Robe rouge, que d'heures proches sous les arbres!
Mais adieu, dans cette aube froide, mon eau pure,
Adieu malgré le cri, l'épaule, le sommeil.

Écoute, il ne faut plus ces mains qui se reprennent
Comme éternellement l'écume et le rocher,
Et même plus ces yeux qui se tournent vers l'ombre,
Aimant mieux le sommeil encore partagé.

Il ne faut plus tenter d'unir voix et prière,
Espoir et nuit, désirs de l'abîme et du port.
Vois, ce n'est pas Mozart qui lutte dans ton âme,
Mais le gong, contre l'arme informe de la mort.

Adieu, visage en mai.
Le bleu du ciel est morne aujourd'hui, ici.
Le glaive de l'indifférence de l'étoile
Blesse une fois de plus la terre du dormeur.

THE TIDE, THE REEF

Solitude, not to be climbed—how many roads!
Red robe—how many hours under the trees!
But farewell, in this cold dawn, my pure water,
Farewell despite the cry, the shoulder, sleep.

Listen: we no longer need these hands that return
To each other, as the tide turns and turns to the rocks
—Not even these eyes that turn toward the shadow,
Preferring that sleep we still share.

We must not strive to join voice and prayer,
Hope and night, desires of the pit and of the harbor.
Look: this isn't Mozart who fights in your soul
But the gong, against the formless sword of death.

Farewell, face in May.
The blue of the sky is dull today, here.
The blade of the star's indifference
Wounds the sleeper's ground once more.

LA LAMPE, LE DORMEUR

I

Je ne savais dormir sans toi, je n'osais pas
Risquer sans toi les marches descendantes.
Plus tard, j'ai découvert que c'est un autre songe,
Cette terre aux chemins qui tombent dans la mort.

Alors je t'ai voulue au chevet de ma fièvre
D'inexister, d'être plus noir que tant de nuit,
Et quand je parlais haut dans le monde inutile,
Je t'avais sur les voies du trop vaste sommeil.

Le dieu pressant en moi, c'étaient ces rives
Que j'éclairais de l'huile errante, et tu sauvais
Nuit après nuit mes pas du gouffre qui m'obsède,
Nuit après nuit mon aube, inachevable amour.

THE LAMP, THE SLEEPER

I

I did not know how to sleep without you, I did not dare
Risk without you the descending steps.
Later I found this was a new dream, this country
Of roads that pitch into death.

Then I wanted you at the bedside of my fever
To not be, to be blacker than so much night;
And when I raised my voice in the useless world
I had you where we walked in the way of too much sleep.

These shores I lit with the drifting oil, they were a god
Urgent in me, and night after night
You saved me from the pit which obsesses me; night after night
Saved my dawn, love that does not reach noon.

— Je me penchais sur toi, vallée de tant de pierres,
J'écoutais les rumeurs de ton grave repos,
J'apercevais très bas dans l'ombre qui te couvre
Le lieu triste où blanchit l'écume du sommeil.

Je t'écoutais rêver. O monotone et sourde,
Et parfois par un roc invisible brisée,
Comme ta voix s'en va, ouvrant parmi ses ombres
Le gave d'une étroite attente murmurée!

Là-haut, dans les jardins de l'émail, il est vrai
Qu'un paon impie s'accroît des lumières mortelles.
Mais toi il te suffit de ma flamme qui bouge,
Tu habites la nuit d'une phrase courbée.

Qui es-tu? Je ne sais de toi que les alarmes,
Les hâtes dans ta voix d'un rite inachevé.
Tu partages l'obscur au sommet de la table,
Et que tes mains sont nues, ô seules éclairées!

II

—I bent over you, valley of so many stones,
I listened to the rumors of your grave repose;
Low in the shadows which cover you
I glimpsed the sad ground where sleep broke into surf.

I listened to you dream. O single-toned and dulled,
Broken at times by an invisible rock, your voice
That slips away murmuringly, how it opens
The torrent of a narrow hope among its shadows!

Above, in the enamel gardens, it is true
An impious peacock swells with the mortal lights.
But my trembling flame is enough for you; you inhabit
The night of a vaulted phrase.

Who are you? I know only your sudden fears,
Your voice hurried in an unfinished rite.
You divide the dark above the table,
And how your hands are bare: in the only light!

Bouche, tu auras bu
A la saveur obscure,
A une eau ensablée,
A l'Être sans retour.

Où vont se réunir
L'eau amère, l'eau douce,
Tu auras bu où brille
L'impartageable amour.

Mais ne t'angoisse pas,
O bouche qui demandes
Plus qu'un reflet troublé
Plus qu'une ombre de jour:

L'âme se fait d'aimer
L'écume sans réponse.
La joie sauve la joie,
L'amour le non-amour.

Mouth, you will have drunk
From the dark savor,
From sandy water, from this
Life without escape.

Where bitter water
And the sweet will gather,
You will have drunk
Where the one love is gleaming.

But don't be alarmed,
O mouth asking more
Than a troubled mirror, more
Than a shadow of day:

The soul spawns itself
Loving the unmindful surf.
Joy saves joy,
Love, what is not love.

33

UNE PIERRE

Il me disait, Tu es une eau, la plus obscure,
La plus fraîche où goûter l'impartageable amour.
J'ai retenu son pas, mais parmi d'autres pierres,
Dans le boire éternel du jour plus bas que jour.

A STONE

He used to say, You are a water, the darkest
And freshest, and here I taste the one love.
I held his steps back, but among other stones,
In the endless flow of the day below all days.

PIERRE ÉCRITE | WORDS IN STONE

Prestige, disais-tu, de notre lampe et des feuillages,
Ces hôtes de nos soirs.
Ils tirent jusqu'à nous leurs barques sur les dalles,
Ils connaissent notre désir de l'éternel.

La nuit parfaite dans le ciel criant son feu,
Eux sont venus d'un pas sans ombre, ils nous éveillent,
Leur parole commence au tremblé de nos voix.

Le pas des astres mesurant le sol dallé de cette nuit,
Et eux mêlant à tant de feux l'obscurité propre de l'homme.

The lure, you said, of our lamp and the leaves,
These hosts of our evenings.
Over the flagstones to our feet they haul their bark,
They know our desire for the eternal.

The night perfect in a sky shouting its fire,
They come with an unshadowed step to wake us,
Their word begins at the trembling of our voices.

The star's pace measures the stone-covered ground of this night,
And they blend man's own darkness with myriad fires.

UNE PIERRE

Il désirait, sans connaître,
Il a péri, sans avoir.
Arbres, fumées,
Toutes lignes de vent et de déception
Furent son gîte.
Infiniment
Il n'a étreint que sa mort.

A STONE

He desired, without knowing.
He perished, without having.
Trees, smoke-trails,
Wind-lines and lines of deception
These were his home.
Again and again he embraced
But only his death.

LE LIEU DES MORTS

Quel est le lieu des morts,
Ont-ils droit comme nous à des chemins,
Parlent-ils, plus réels étant leurs mots,
Sont-ils l'esprit des feuillages ou des feuillages plus hauts?

Phénix a-t-il construit pour eux un château,
Dressé pour eux une table?
Le cri de quelque oiseau dans le feu de quelque arbre
Est-il l'espace où ils se pressent tous?

Peut-être gisent-ils dans la feuille du lierre,
Leur parole défaite
Étant le port de la déchirure des feuilles, où la nuit vient.

THE PLACE OF THE DEAD

What is the place of the dead—
Do they have a right, as we do, to roads—
Do they speak—are their words more real—
Are they the spirit of these leaves, or of a higher foliage?

Did the phoenix build a castle for them—
Did he set their table?
A bird's cry in the fire of a tree—
Is that the space they all crowd in?

Here the dead may lie, in the ivy leaf
—Their ruined word
The harbor, the torn leaf, where the night comes in.

UNE PIERRE

Je fus assez belle.
Il se peut qu'un jour comme celui-ci me ressemble.
Mais la ronce l'emporte sur mon visage,
La pierre accable mon corps.

Approche-toi,
Servante verticale rayée de noir,
Et ton visage court.

Répands le lait ténébreux, qui exalte
Ma force simple.
Sois-moi fidèle,
Nourrice encor, mais d'immortalité.

A STONE

I was pretty enough.
A day like this could resemble me.
But thorns cover my face,
And stone crushes my body.

Come closer
Straight-backed servant, you who are streaked with black,
And your short face—

Pour out the night's milk, it exalts
My simple force.
Stay with me,
Wetnurse still, but feeding me immortality.

LE LIEU DES MORTS

Le lieu des morts,
C'est peut-être le pli de l'étoffe rouge.
Peut-être tombent-ils
Dans ses mains rocailleuses; s'aggravent-ils
Dans les touffes en mer de la couleur rouge;
Ont-ils comme miroir
Le corps gris de la jeune aveugle; ont-ils pour faim
Dans le chant des oiseaux ses mains de noyée.

Ou sont-ils réunis sous le sycomore ou l'érable?
Nul bruit ne trouble plus leur assemblée.
La déesse se tient au sommet de l'arbre,
Elle incline vers eux l'aiguière d'or.

Et seul parfois le bras divin brille dans l'arbre
Et des oiseaux se taisent, d'autres oiseaux.

THE PLACE OF THE DEAD

The place of the dead—
Perhaps it is a fold in the red cloth.
Perhaps the dead fall
Into the rough hands of the cloth; or are they worn down
By wisps of red at sea;
Or have they the grey body
Of the blind girl as a mirror; or have they her hands
Drowned in the birds' song, as their hunger?

Or do they meet under the sycamore or the maple?
No sound troubles their company now.
The goddess stays at the top of the tree,
She offers them the golden ewer.

And at times the divine arm shines alone in the tree,
And a few birds are still, in other worlds.

UNE PIERRE

Deux ans, ou trois,
Je me sentis suffisante. Les astres,
Les fleuves, les forêts ne m'égalaient pas.
La lune s'écaillait sur mes robes grises.
Mes yeux cernés
Illuminaient les mers sous leurs voûtes d'ombre,
Et mes cheveux étaient plus amples que ce monde
Aux yeux vaincus, aux cris qui ne m'atteignaient pas.

Des bêtes de nuit hurlent, c'est mon chemin,
Des portes noires se ferment.

A STONE

For two years, or three
I was enough in myself. Stars,
Streams, forests did not equal me.
The moon scaled on my grey robes.
My dark-circled eyes
Lit the seas beneath their shadowed arches,
And my hair spread wider than all this world
With its vanquished eyes, with its cries that could not reach me.

Night-beasts howl, and that is my road now;
And black doors close.

UNE PIERRE

Ta jambe, nuit très dense,
Tes seins, liés,
Si noirs, ai-je perdu mes yeux,
Mes nerfs d'atroce vue
Dans cette obscurité plus âpre que la pierre,
O mon amour?

Au centre de la lumière, j'abolis
D'abord ma tête crevassée par le gaz,
Mon nom ensuite avec tous pays,
Mes mains seules droites persistent.

En tête du cortège je suis tombé
Sans dieu, sans voix audible, sans péché,
Bête trinitaire criante.

50

A STONE

Your leg, dense night
—Your bound breasts—
So black, have I lost my eyes
In this dark more galling than stone
—O my love
Lost my foul-sighted nerves?

At the light's center, I abolish first
My face pocked by the gas
And then my name along with all countries;
My hands hold on alone.

Godless, voiceless, sinless—
At the head of the column I fell,
A shouting three-headed beast.

UNE PIERRE

Tombe, mais douce pluie, sur le visage.
Éteins, mais lentement, le très pauvre chaleil.

A STONE

Fall, but with soft rain, on this face.
Put the poor lamp out slowly.

JEAN ET JEANNE

Tu demandes le nom
De cette maison basse délabrée,
C'est Jean et Jeanne en un autre pays.

Quand les larges vents passent
Le seuil où rien ne chante ni paraît.

C'est Jean et Jeanne et de leurs faces grises
Le plâtre du jour tombe et je revois
La vitre des étés anciens. Te souviens-tu?
La plus brillante au loin, l'arche fille des ombres.

Aujourd'hui, ce soir, nous ferons un feu
Dans la grande salle.
Nous nous éloignerons,
Nous le laisserons vivre pour les morts.

JOHN AND JOAN

You ask the name
Of this battered one-story house—
It's John and Joan in another land.

When the broad winds pass the threshold
Where nothing sings or comes to light—

It's John and Joan and the day's plaster falls
From their grey faces, and I see again
The window of past summers. Do you remember?
Far off the most brilliant, the ark, daughter of shadows.

Today, this evening, we'll build a fire
In the great room.
We will retreat,
We will let it live for the dead.

UNE PIERRE

Aglaure s'est dressée
Dans les feuilles mortes.
Sa taille enfiévrée s'est reformée
Sous des mains diligentes.
Sa nuque s'est ployée sous la chaleur des lèvres.
La nuit vint, qui couvrit sa face dévastée
Et ses sanglots épars dans le lit de la glaise.

A STONE

Aglauros stood upright
Among the dead leaves.
Her fevered waist was reshaped
By diligent hands.
The heat of lips bent her neck.
Night came to cover her ravaged face
And the sobs she'd scattered over the clay bed.

UNE PIERRE

Longtemps dura l'enfance au mur sombre et je fus
La conscience d'hiver; qui se pencha
Tristement, fortement, sur une image,
Amèrement, sur le reflet d'un autre jour.

N'ayant rien désiré
Plus que de contribuer à mêler deux lumières,
O mémoire, je fus
Dans son vaisseau de verre l'huile diurne
Criant son âme rouge au ciel des longues pluies.

Qu'aurai-je aimé? L'écume de la mer
Au-dessus de Trieste, quand le gris
De la mer de Trieste éblouissait
Les yeux du sphinx déchirable des rives.

A STONE

It was a long childhood by the dark wall, and I was
Winter's conscience: bent
Sadly, strongly over an image; bitterly
Over the reflection of another day.

Wanting nothing more
Than to help blend two strains of light,
I was (o memory)
The oil burning by day in its lamp of glass,
Shouting its red soul to the long-rained sky.

What will I have loved? The sea-spume
Above Trieste, when the grey
Of the sea at Trieste dazzled
The eyes of the brittle shore-bound sphinx.

UNE PIERRE

Orages puis orages je ne fus
Qu'un chemin de la terre.
Mais les pluies apaisaient l'inapaisable terre,
Mourir a fait le lit de la nuit dans mon coeur.

A STONE

Storms and more storms—I was no more
Than a road on the earth.
But the rains quenched the unquenchable earth,
And dying has made my heart the bed of night.

UNE PIERRE

Le livre de Porphyre sur le soleil,
Regarde-le tel qu'un amas de pierres noires.
J'ai lu longtemps le livre de Porphyre,
Je suis venu au lieu de nul soleil.

A STONE

The book of Porphyry on the sun—
Look at it as a mound of black stones.
After reading Porphyry's book for a long time
I came to the place where there is no sun.

UNE PIERRE

O dite à demi-voix parmi les branches,
O murmurée, ô tue,
Porteuse d'éternel, lune, entr'ouvre les grilles
Et penche-toi pour nous qui n'avons plus de jour.

A STONE

You whom we name in a low voice among the branches,
You who are murmured, who are kept dark,
Who bring the eternal: moon, half open the gate
And favor us who have no more day.

La face la plus sombre a crié
Que le jour est proche.
En vain le buis s'est-il resserré
Sur le vieux jardin.

Ce peuple aussi a sa plainte,
Cette absence, son espoir,
Mais la lune se couvre et l'ombre
Emplit la bouche des morts.

The darkest face cried
That day is near.
In vain the box-tree tightened
Its grip on the old garden.

Yes, this people has its sorrow,
This absence, its hope.
But the moon is clouded and shadow
Fills the mouth of the dead.

SUR UN ÉROS DE BRONZE

Tu vieillissais dans les plis
De la grisaille divine.
Qui est venu, d'une lampe,
Empourprer ton horizon nu?

L'enfant sans hâte ni bruit
T'a découvert une route.
— Ce n'est pas que l'antique nuit
En toi ne s'angoisse plus.

Le même enfant volant bas
Dans la ténèbre des voûtes
A saisi ce coeur et l'emporte
Dans le feuillage inconnu.

ON A BRONZE EROS

You had grown old
In the divine folds of no color.
Who came with a lamp
To redden your bare horizon?

The noiseless child, motionless
Has found a road for you.
—Not that the antique night
Does not still seethe in you.

The same child flying low
Through the same shadow of arches
Has seized this heart and has carried it off
Into the unknown foliage.

UNE VOIX

Nous vieillissions, lui le feuillage et moi la source,
Lui le peu de soleil et moi la profondeur,
Et lui la mort et moi la sagesse de vivre.

J'acceptais que le temps nous présentât dans l'ombre
Son visage de faune au rire non moqueur,
J'aimais que se levât le vent qui porte l'ombre

Et que mourir ne fût en obscure fontaine
Que troubler l'eau sans fond que le lierre buvait.
J'aimais, j'étais debout dans le songe éternel.

A VOICE

We were growing old, he the foliage and myself the source;
He the bit of sun and myself the depths;
He who is death and myself the wisdom of living.

I accepted when time showed his face
Like a faun's, laughing without mockery in the shadow;
I loved that the wind rises, carrying the shadow;

And that death did no more than trouble the soundless water
In the dark fountain where the ivy drank.
I loved, I stood upright in the eternal dream.

UN FEU VA DEVANT NOUS | A FIRE GOES BEFORE US

LA CHAMBRE

Le miroir et le fleuve en crue, ce matin,
S'appelaient à travers la chambre, deux lumières
Se trouvent et s'unissent dans l'obscur
Des meubles de la chambre descellée.

Et nous étions deux pays de sommeil
Communiquant par leurs marches de pierre
Où se perdait l'eau non trouble d'un rêve
Toujours se reformant, toujours brisé.

La main pure dormait près de la main soucieuse.
Un corps un peu parfois dans son rêve bougeait.
Et loin, sur l'eau plus noire d'une table,
La robe rouge éclairante dormait.

THE BEDROOM

The mirror and the flooding stream, this morning,
Called to each other across the room: two lights
Meeting and marrying among the shadowed
Fixtures of the unsealed room.

And we were two lands of sleep
Sharing a common border of stone
Where untroubled water slipped away, a dream
Forming again, again broken.

The pure hand slept by the careworn.
At times a body stirred in its dreaming.
Far off, on the blacker waters of a table,
The red robe slept in its own light.

L'ÉPAULE

Ton épaule soit l'aube, ayant porté
Tout mon obscur déchirement de nuit
Et toute cette écume amère des images,
Tout ce haut rougeoiement d'un impossible été.

Ton corps voûte pour nous son heure respirante
Comme un pays plus clair sur nos ombres penché
— Longue soit la journée où glisse, miroitante,
L'eau d'un rêve à l'afflux rapide, irrévélé.

O dans le bruissement du feuillage de l'arbre
Soit le masque aux yeux clos du rêve déposé!
J'entends déjà grandir le bruit d'un autre gave
Qui s'apaise, ou se perd, dans notre éternité.

THE SHOULDER

May your shoulder be the dawn, having carried
By night my dark laceration
And this bitter spume of images,
This impossible summer, this reddening high over the trees.

May your body arch for us its breathing hour
Like a brighter land bent over our shadows
—May that day be long when the shimmering dream
Glides like running water, unrevealed.

O, in the rustling of the tree's foliage
May the shut-eye mask of the dream be left!
Already I hear the sound grow of another stream
That is appeased, or lost, in our eternity.

L'ARBRE, LA LAMPE

L'arbre vieillit dans l'arbre, c'est l'été.
L'oiseau franchit le chant de l'oiseau et s'évade.
Le rouge de la robe illumine et disperse
Loin, au ciel, le charroi de l'antique douleur.

O fragile pays,
Comme la flamme d'une lampe que l'on porte,
Proche étant le sommeil dans la sève du monde,
Simple le battement de l'âme partagée.

Toi aussi tu aimes l'instant où la lumière des lampes
Se décolore et rêve dans le jour.
Tu sais que c'est l'obscur de ton coeur qui guérit,
La barque qui rejoint le rivage et tombe.

THE TREE, THE LAMP

The tree grows old within the tree—it is summer.
The bird flies over the birdsong and escapes.
Far off in the sky, the red of the robe illumines
And disperses the chariots of the antique sorrow.

O fragile land
Like the flame of the lamp we carry;
Now in the world's sap, sleep is near
And simple now the undoubled beat of the soul.

You too, you love the moment when the lamps' light
Discolors, and dreams in the day.
You know it's the dark in your heart that's recovering
And the boat that rejoins the shore, and that falls.

LES CHEMINS

Chemins, parmi
La matière des arbres. Dieux, parmi
Les touffes de ce chant inlassable d'oiseaux.
Et tout ton sang voûté sous une main rêveuse,
O proche, ô tout mon jour.

Qui ramassa le fer
Rouillé, parmi les hautes herbes, n'oublie plus
Qu'aux grumeaux du métal la lumière peut prendre
Et consumer le sel du doute et de la mort.

THE ROADS

Roads, through
The matter of trees. Gods, through
The wisps of this tireless birdsong.
And all your blood arched under a dreaming hand,
O you who are close, o all my day.

Whoever found the rusty
Iron in the high grass, no longer forgets
That the light can flame on the clotted metal,
And consume there the salt of doubt and of death.

LE MYRTE

Parfois je te savais la terre, je buvais
Sur tes lèvres l'angoisse des fontaines
Quand elle sourd des pierres chaudes, et l'été
Dominait haut la pierre heureuse et le buveur.

Parfois je te disais de myrte et nous brûlions
L'arbre de tous tes gestes tout un jour.
C'étaient de grands feux brefs de lumière vestale,
Ainsi je t'inventais parmi tes cheveux clairs.

Tout un grand été nul avait séché nos rêves,
Rouillé nos voix, accru nos corps, défait nos fers.
Parfois le lit tournait comme une barque libre
Qui gagne lentement le plus haut de la mer.

THE MYRTLE

At times I knew you were the earth, and I drank
From your lips when anguish surged in fountains
From the warm stones, and summer
Rose above the happy stone and the drinker.

At times I called you the myrtle, and all of a day passed
In burning the tree of all your gestures.
Those were the large, momentary fires of vestal light
—So I invented you in your bright hair.

For a great empty summer had dried our dreams,
Rusted our voices, enlarged our bodies, unlocked our chains.
At times the bed turned like a small boat cut free
And slowly gaining the high seas.

LE SANG, LA NOTE SI

Longues, longues journées.
Le sang inapaisé heurte le sang.
Le nageur est aveugle.
Il descend par étages pourpres dans le battement de ton coeur.

Quand la nuque se tend
Le cri toujours désert prend une bouche pure.

Ainsi vieillit l'été. Ainsi la mort
Encercle le bonheur de la flamme qui bouge.
Et nous dormons un peu. La note si
Résonne très longtemps dans l'étoffe rouge.

THE BLOOD, THE NOTE B

Long, long days.
The unappeased blood thrusts against the blood.
The swimmer is blind.
He sinks through crimson strata in the beating of your heart.

When the neck tautens
The bare cry takes a pure mouth.

So the summer ages. So death
Encircles the gladness of the moving flame.
And we sleep a little. The note B
Echoes and re-echoes in the red cloth.

L'ABEILLE, LA COULEUR

Cinq heures.
Le sommeil est léger, en taches sur les vitres.
Le jour puise là-bas dans la couleur l'eau fraîche,
Ruisselante, du soir.

Et c'est comme si l'âme se simplifie
Étant lumière davantage, et qui rassure,
Mais, l'Un se déchirant contre la jambe obscure,
Tu te perds, où la bouche a bu à l'âcre mort.

(La corne d'abondance avec le fruit
Rouge dans le soleil qui tourne. Et tout ce bruit
D'abeilles de l'impure et douce éternité
Sur le si proche pré si brûlant encore).

THE BEE, THE COLOR

Five o'clock.
A light sleep dapples the windows.
Day draws the fresh and rustling water of evening
From that well of color.

And it is as if the soul is simpler,
Filled with a reassuring light;
But One is torn on the dark leg
And you lose yourself where the mouth drank acrid death.

(The cornucopia with the red fruit
In the turning sun. And all this noise
Of bees swarming from the still flaming meadow,
As if a sweet impure eternity were near us.)

LE SOIR

Rayures bleues et noires.
Un labour qui dévie vers le bas du ciel.
Le lit, vaste et brisé comme le fleuve en crue.
— Vois, c'est déjà le soir,
Et le feu parle auprès de nous dans l'éternité de la sauge.

THE EVENING

Blue and black furrows.
A field that turns aside at the foot of the sky.
The bed, vast and broken like the flooding river.
—Look, it is already evening; and near us
The fire talks in the eternity of the sage leaf.

LA LUMIÈRE DU SOIR

Le soir,
Ces oiseaux qui se parlent, indéfinis,
Qui se mordent, lumière.
La main qui a bougé sur le flanc désert.

Nous sommes immobiles depuis longtemps.
Nous parlons bas.
Et le temps reste autour de nous comme des flaques
    de couleur.

THE LIGHT OF EVENING

Evening.
These birds, indefinite; their voices,
Biting; and the light.
The hand which moved on the bare flank.

We have not moved in a long time.
We speak softly.
And time lies in pools of color around us.

LA PATIENCE, LE CIEL

Que te faut-il, voix qui reprends, proche du sol comme la sève
De l'olivier que glaça l'autre hiver?
Le temps divin qu'il faut pour emplir ce vase,
Oui, rien qu'aimer ce temps désert et plein de jour.

La patience pour faire vivre un feu sous un ciel rapide,
L'attente indivisée pour un vin noir,
L'heure aux arches ouvertes quand le vent
A des ombres qui rouent sur tes mains pensives.

PATIENCE, SKY

What do you need? (Voice you spring up again, close to the earth
As the sap of the olive tree frozen last winter.)
The divine time to fill this vase;
Yes, nothing more than to love this bare time filled with day.

The patience to breathe life into a fire under a rapid sky;
The undivided wait for a black wine;
The hour and its open arches when the wind's
Shadows roll on your pensive hands.

UNE VOIX

Combien simples, oh fûmes-nous, parmi ces branches,
Inexistants, allant du même pas,
Une ombre aimant une ombre, et l'espace des branches
Ne criant pas du poids d'ombres, ne bougeant pas.

Je t'avais converti aux sommeils sans alarmes,
Aux pas sans lendemains, aux jours sans devenir,
A l'effraie aux buissons quand la nuit claire tombe,
Tournant vers nous ses yeux de terre sans retour.

A mon silence; à mes angoisses sans tristesse
Où tu cherchais le goût du temps qui va mûrir.
A de grands chemins clos, où venait boire l'astre
Immobile d'aimer, de prendre et de mourir.

A VOICE

How simple we were among these branches:
Unalive, the two of us walking with one step;
One shadow loving another; and the branches
Not crying out under the weight of shadows, not even moving.

I had converted you to a fearless sleep,
To steps outside time, to unmoving days
And when the clear night falls, to the owl in the bushes
Turning toward us his eyes filled with the earth of no escape.

To my silence; to my anguish without sadness
In which you sought the taste of ripening time.
To great closed roads where the unmoving star came to drink
—The star of loving, of grasping and of dying.

UNE PIERRE

Un feu va devant nous.
J'aperçois par instants ta nuque, ton visage,
Puis, rien que le flambeau,
Rien que le feu massif, le mascaret des morts.

Cendre qui te détaches de la flamme
Dans la lumière du soir,
O présence,
Sous ta voûte furtive accueille-nous
Pour une fête obscure.

A STONE

A fire goes before us.
For a moment I glimpsed your nape, your face,
And then only the torch,
Only the massive fire, the surge of the dead.

Ember, you who fall away from the flame
In the evening light,
O presence:
Gather us under your furtive arch
For a dark celebration.

LA LUMIÈRE, CHANGÉE

Nous ne nous voyons plus dans la même lumière,
Nous n'avons plus les mêmes yeux, les mêmes mains.
L'arbre est plus proche et la voix des sources plus vive,
Nos pas sont plus profonds, parmi les morts.

Dieu qui n'es pas, pose ta main sur notre épaule,
Ébauche notre corps du poids de ton retour,
Achève de mêler à nos âmes ces astres,
Ces bois, ces cris d'oiseaux, ces ombres et ces jours.

Renonce-toi en nous comme un fruit se déchire,
Efface-nous en toi. Découvre-nous
Le sens mystérieux de ce qui n'est que simple
Et fût tombé sans feu dans des mots sans amour.

THE SAME LIGHT, CHANGED

We no longer see each other in the same light;
We no longer have the same eyes, the same hands.
The tree is closer and the river's voice more lively;
Our steps sink deeper, among the dead.

God who is not, put your hand on our shoulder
And rough-cast our bodies from the weight of your return.
Still blend our souls with these stars,
Woods, these bird-cries, shadows, these days.

Renounce yourself in us, as a fruit tears itself apart;
Dissolve us in you. Unfold for us
The mysterious sense of what is only simple,
Or what would have fallen without fire,
    had words been without love.

UNE PIERRE

Le jour au fond du jour sauvera-t-il
Le peu de mots que nous fûmes ensemble?
Pour moi, j'ai tant aimé ces jours confiants, je veille
Sur quelques mots éteints dans l'âtre de nos coeurs.

A STONE

Will the day underlying the day
Save the few words that we were together?
As for myself, I so much loved those trusting days; now I keep
Vigil over a few extinct words in the hearth of our hearts.

UNE PIERRE

Nous prenions par ces prés
Où parfois tout un dieu se détachait d'un arbre
(Et c'était notre preuve, vers le soir).

Je vous poussais sans bruit,
Je sentais votre poids contre nos mains pensives,
O vous, mes mots obscurs,
Barrières au travers des chemins du soir.

A STONE

We used to cross these fields
Where at times an entire god fell away from the tree
(And towards evening this was our proof)

I pushed you noiselessly,
I felt your weight against our pensive hands
—O you, my dark words,
Barriers across the evening roads.

LE COEUR, L'EAU NON TROUBLÉE

Es-tu gaie ou triste?
— Ai-je su jamais,
Sauf que rien ne pèse
Au coeur sans retour.

Aucun pas d'oiseau
Sur cette verrière
Du coeur traversé
De jardins et d'ombre.

Un souci de toi
Qui a bu ma vie
Mais dans ce feuillage
Aucun souvenir.

Je suis l'heure simple
Et l'eau non troublée.
Ai-je su t'aimer,
Ne sachant mourir?

THE HEART, THE UNTROUBLED WATER

Are you gay or sad?
—Did I ever know,
Save that nothing weighs
On the unreturning heart.

Not one bird
Steps on this skylight
—This heart shot through
With gardens and shadow.

Concern for you
Drank my life,
But not one memory
In this foliage.

I am the simple hour
And the untroubled water.
Did I know to love you,
Not knowing enough to die?

LA PAROLE DU SOIR

Le pays du début d'octobre n'avait fruit
Qui ne se déchirât dans l'herbe, et ses oiseaux
En venaient à des cris d'absence et de rocaille
Sur un haut flanc courbé qui se hâtait vers nous.

Ma parole du soir,
Comme un raisin d'arrière-automne tu as froid,
Mais le vin déjà brûle en ton âme et je trouve
Ma seule chaleur vraie dans tes mots fondateurs.

Le vaisseau d'un achèvement d'octobre, clair,
Peut venir. Nous saurons mêler ces deux lumières,
O mon vaisseau illuminé errant en mer,

Clarté de proche nuit et clarté de parole,
— Brume qui montera de toute chose vive
Et toi, mon rougeoiement de lampe dans la mort.

THE WORD OF EVENING

The land of early October was left with fruit
That rotted in the grass, and all its birds
At last cried out absence and rock
From a high curved flank that was hurrying toward us.

My word of evening,
You are cold as a grape from the end of autumn
But already the wine burns in your soul, and I find
My only true heat in your founding words.

The clear ship may come
Of an October consummation. We will still know
    how to blend these two lights,
O my bright wandering ship on the sea,

Clarity of near-night, clarity of the word
—Mist which will rise from all living things
And you, in death my lamp's ruddy glow.

«ANDIAM, COMPAGNE BELLE . . .»

Don Giovanni, I, 3.

Les lampes de la nuit passée, dans le feuillage,
Brûlent-elles encor, et dans quel pays?
C'est le soir, où l'arbre s'aggrave, sur la porte.
L'étoile a précédé le frêle feu mortel.

Andiam, compagne belle, astres, demeures,
Rivière plus brillante avec le soir.
J'entends tomber sur vous, qu'une musique emporte,
L'écume où bat le coeur introuvable des morts.

"ANDIAM, COMPAGNE BELLE . . ."

Don Giovanni, I, 3.

Are the lamps that burned in the leaves last night
Still burning? And in what country?
It is evening, and the tree grows more dense at the door.
The star was here before the frail and mortal fire.

Andiam, compagne belle; stars, houses of heaven,
And you, river more brilliant with evening.
I hear breaking on you who fade like music
The foam in which beats the dead's unmeasured heart.

LE LIVRE, POUR VIEILLIR

Étoiles transhumantes; et le berger
Voûté sur le bonheur terrestre; et tant de paix
Comme ce cri d'insecte, irrégulier,
Qu'un dieu pauvre façonne. Le silence
Est monté de ton livre vers ton coeur.
Un vent bouge sans bruit dans les bruits du monde.
Le temps sourit au loin de cesser d'être.
Simples dans le verger sont les fruits mûrs.

Tu vieilliras
Et, te décolorant dans la couleur des arbres,
Faisant ombre plus lente sur le mur,
Étant, et d'âme enfin, la terre menacée,
Tu reprendras le livre à la page laissée,
Tu diras, C'étaient donc les derniers mots obscurs.

THE BOOK, TO GROW OLD WITH

Transhumant stars; and the shepherd
Arched over all earthly joy; and such peace
As this insect's uneven cry
Fashioned by an impoverished god. Silence
Rose from your book to your heart.
A wind moves noiselessly in the world's noise.
Far off, time smiles and is no longer.
And ripe fruit is simple in the grove.

You will grow old
And, fading against the color of the trees,
Casting a slower shadow on the wall,
Yourself the menaced earth: body and, at long last, soul;
You will take up the book where you had left it,
And say, "So those were the last difficult words."

LE DIALOGUE D'ANGOISSE ET DE DÉSIR

THE DIALOGUE BETWEEN ANGUISH AND DESIRE

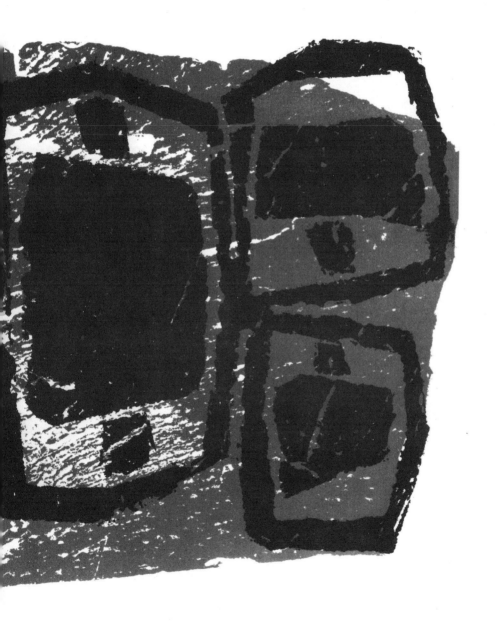

I

J'imagine souvent, au-dessus de moi,
Un visage sacrificiel, dont les rayons
Sont comme un champ de terre labourée.
Les lèvres et les yeux sont souriants,
Le front est morne, un bruit de mer lassant et sourd.
Je lui dis : Sois ma force, et sa lumière augmente,
Il domine un pays de guerre au petit jour
Et tout un fleuve qui rassure par méandres
Cette terre saisie fertilisée.

Et je m'étonne alors qu'il ait fallu
Ce temps, et cette peine. Car les fruits
Régnaient déjà dans l'arbre. Et le soleil
Illuminait déjà le pays du soir.
Je regarde les hauts plateaux où je puis vivre,
Cette main qui retient une autre main rocheuse
Cette respiration d'absence qui soulève
Les masses d'un labour d'automne inachevé

I

Often I imagine a sacrificial face
Above me, whose rays of light
Are like a tilled field.
The lips and eyes are smiling, and the forehead
Is disconsolate, a heavy flat sound of the sea.
I say: "Be my force;" and his light grows;
At dawn he rises over a land at war
And over a long meandering river which reassures
This land that is now seized and fertilized.

And now I am surprised that all this time
And hardship were needed. For the fruit
Already reigned in the tree. And the sun
Was already shining on the evening land.
I look at the high plains where I can live,
And at this hand that holds another hand of stone,
And at this breath of absence, lifting
The earth in autumn: the unfinished plowing.

II

Et je pense à Coré l'absente; qui a pris
Dans ses mains le coeur noir étincelant des fleurs
Et qui tomba, buvant le noir, l'irrévélée,
Sur le pré de lumière — et d'ombre. Je comprends
Cette faute, la mort. Asphodèles, jasmins
Sont de notre pays. Des rives d'eau
Peu profonde et limpide et verte y font frémir
L'ombre du coeur du monde... Mais oui, prends.
La faute de la fleur coupée nous est remise,
Toute l'âme se voûte autour d'un dire simple,
La grisaille se perd dans le fruit mûr.

Le fer des mots de guerre se dissipe
Dans l'heureuse matière sans retour.

II

And I think of Kore who was lost; who has grasped
The black spangly hearts of the flowers
And has fallen, unrevealed, drinking the dark
On the field of light—and of shadow. I understand
This sin, death. Asphodels, jasmine,
These are of our land. Here the rivers
—Limpid and green, not very deep—
Stir the shadow of the world's heart . . . Yes, accept.
The sin of the cut flower is taken from us;
The entire soul arches over a few simple words;
The grisaille is lost in the ripe fruit.

The iron of the words of war
Dissolves in the joy of what is earth.

III

Oui, c'est cela.
Un éblouissement dans les mots anciens.
L'étagement
De toute notre vie au loin comme une mer
Heureuse, élucidée par une arme d'eau vive.

Nous n'avons plus besoin
D'images déchirantes pour aimer.
Cet arbre nous suffit, là-bas, qui, par lumière,
Se délie de soi-même et ne sait plus
Que le nom presque dit d'un dieu presque incarné.

Et tout ce haut pays que l'Un très proche brûle,

Et ce crépi d'un mur que le temps simple touche
De ses mains sans tristesse, et qui ont mesuré.

III

Yes, that's it.
A flame in the words that came before.
The layering
Of our life, as a blade of running water
Clarifies a glad sea.

We can love now
Without the rending images.
For us that tree is enough
Which separates from itself in the light, and knows nothing
But the almost spoken name of an almost incarnate god.

And all this high land that the near One burns,

And the wall's plaster, touched by the simple time,
Whose hands have measured, and are not sad.

IV

Et toi,
Et c'est là mon orgueil,
O moins à contre-jour, ô mieux aimée,
Qui ne m'es plus étrangère. Nous avons grandi, je le sais,
Dans les mêmes jardins obscurs. Nous avons bu
La même eau difficile sous les arbres.
Le même ange sévère t'a menacée.

Et nos pas sont les mêmes, se déprenant
Des ronces de l'enfance oubliable et des mêmes
Imprécations impures.

IV

And you
—And here is all my pride—
And in this light you are less obscure, my more truly
Loved, you are no longer strange to me. Yes, we have grown
In the same dark gardens. We have drunk
The same difficult water beneath the trees.
The same harsh angel has threatened you.

And our steps match, as they clear themselves
From the brambles of a forgettable childhood, and from the same
Impure curses.

V

Imagine qu'un soir
La lumière s'attarde sur la terre,
Ouvrant ses mains d'orage et donatrices, dont
La paume est notre lieu et d'angoisse et d'espoir.
Imagine que la lumière soit victime
Pour le salut d'un lieu mortel et sous un dieu
Certes distant et noir. L'après-midi
A été pourpre et d'un trait simple. Imaginer
S'est déchiré dans le miroir, tournant vers nous
Sa face souriante d'argent clair.
Et nous avons vieilli un peu. Et le bonheur
A mûri ses fruits clairs en d'absentes ramures.
Est-ce là un pays plus proche, mon eau pure?
Ces chemins que tu vas dans d'ingrates paroles
Vont-ils sur une rive à jamais ta demeure
«Au loin» prendre musique, «au soir» se dénouer?

V

Imagine that one evening
The light pauses on the earth,
Opening stormy generous hands, whose palms
Are our place both of anguish and of hope.
Imagine the light a victim
For the sake of a mortal ground, under a god
Who is (of course) distant and dark. The afternoon
Was crimson, its features simple. Imagining
Dissolved in the mirror, turning toward us
A smiling face of bright silver.
And we grew a little older. And joy
Ripened its fruit on missing branches.
Is that a nearer land, my pure water?
Will these roads where you walked among harsh words
"Far off" become music, on that shore
Which is yours forever, and "at night" be untied?

VI

O de ton aile de terre et d'ombre éveille-nous,
Ange vaste comme la terre, et porte-nous
Ici, au même endroit de la terre mortelle,
Pour un commencement. Les fruits anciens
Soient notre faim et notre soif enfin calmées.
Le feu soit notre feu. Et l'attente se change
En ce proche destin, cette heure, ce séjour.

Le fer, blé absolu,
Ayant germé dans la jachère de nos gestes,
De nos malédictions, de nos mains pures,
Étant tombé en grains qui ont accueilli l'or
D'un temps, comme le cercle des astres proches,
Et bienveillant et nul,

Ici, où nous allons,
Où nous avons appris l'universel langage,

Ouvre-toi, parle-nous, déchire-toi,
Couronne incendiée, battement clair,
Ambre du coeur solaire.

VI

O wake us with your wing of earth and shadow,
Angel vast like the earth; and carry us
Here, to the same place on the mortal earth,
For a beginning. May the ancient fruit
Calm our hunger at last, and our thirst.
May this fire be our fire. And may the waiting turn
Into this fate at hand, this hour, this place.

Iron, the perfect wheat,
Having seeded in the fallow-land of our gestures,
Of our curses, of our pure hands;
Having fallen in grains which gathered the gold
Of a time—beneficent and barren,
As if it were the circle of nearby stars;

Here, where we walk,
Where we have learned the universal language,

Open up, speak to us, tear yourself apart:
Gutted crown, clear amber
Beating in the solar heart.

SUR UNE PIETA DE TINTORET

Jamais douleur
Ne fut plus élégante dans ces grilles
Noires, que dévora le soleil. Et jamais
Élégance ne fut cause plus spirituelle,
Un feu double, debout sur les grilles du soir.

Ici,
Un grand espoir fut peintre. Oh, qui est plus réel
Du chagrin désirant ou de l'image peinte?
Le désir déchira le voile de l'image,
L'image donna vie à l'exsangue désir.

ON A PIETA BY TINTORETTO

Grief was never
More elegant behind this black
Gate, that the sun devoured. And elegance
Was never a more spiritual cause:
A double flame, settling on the gates at night.

Here
A great hope was the painter. Oh which is more real
—The hungering sorrow or the painted icon?
Hunger tore the icon's veil,
The icon quickened the bloodless hunger.

UNE VOIX

Toi que l'on dit qui bois de cette eau presque absente,
Souviens-toi qu'elle nous échappe et parle-nous.
La décevante est-elle, enfin saisie,
D'un autre goût que l'eau mortelle et seras-tu
L'illuminé d'une obscure parole
Bue à cette fontaine et toujours vive,
Ou l'eau n'est-elle qu'ombre, où ton visage
Ne fait que réfléchir sa finitude?
— Je ne sais pas, je ne suis plus, le temps s'achève
Comme la crue d'un rêve aux dieux irrévélés,
Et ta voix, comme une eau elle-même, s'efface
De ce langage clair et qui m'a consumé.
Oui, je puis vivre ici. L'ange, qui est la terre,
Va dans chaque buisson et paraître et brûler.
Je suis cet autel vide, et ce gouffre, et ces arches
Et toi-même peut-être, et le doute: mais l'aube
Et le rayonnement de pierres descellées.

A VOICE

They say you drink from this water that is almost gone:
Then remember that it escapes us, and speak to us.
Once seized, will the elusive one
Taste different than our mortal water, and will you be
Witness to a dark word
Drunk from that fountain, and still alive;
Or is the water only shadow, and does your face
Only reflect there its limitation?
—I don't know, I am no more, time is ending
As a dream filled with the unrevealed gods
Rises. And, itself like the water, your voice fades
From these bright words that consumed me.
Yes, I can live here. The angel, who is the earth,
Enters each bush, to appear there and burn.
I am the empty altar, and this pit, and these arches
And maybe you, too, and the doubt: but certainly the dawn
And the resplendence of the unsealed stones.

ART DE LA POÉSIE

Dragué fut le regard hors de cette nuit.
Immobilisées et séchées les mains.
On a réconcilié la fièvre. On a dit au coeur
D'être le coeur. Il y avait un démon dans ces veines
Qui s'est enfui en criant.
Il y avait dans la bouche une voix morne sanglante
Qui a été lavée et rappelée.

THE ART OF POETRY

The eyes outside this night were dredged.
The hands, immobilized and warmed.
The fever was reconciled, and the heart told
To be the heart. There was a demon in these veins
Who fled, screaming.
There was a bloody disconsolate voice in the mouth,
It was washed and called forth.

Selected Bibliography

Works by Bonnefoy

Du mouvement et de l'immobilité de Douve. Paris: Mercure de France, 1953. Translated by Galway Kinnell as *On the Motion and Immobility of Douve.* Athens, Ohio: Ohio University Press, 1968 (poetry).

Hier regnant Désert. Paris: Mercure de France, 1958 (poetry).

Pierre écrite. Paris: Mercure de France, 1965 (poetry).

Dans le leurre du seuil. Paris: Mercure de France, 1975 (poetry).

L'Improbable. Paris: Mercure de France, 1959 (essays).

Rome 1630, l'horizon du premier baroque. Paris: Flammarion, 1970 (art).

L'Arrière-pays. Geneva: Skira, 1972 (poetic autobiography).

Un rêve fait à Mantoue. Paris: Mercure de France, 1967 (essays).

Arthur Rimbaud. Paris: Éditions du Seuil, 1961. Translated by Paul Smith. New York: Harper and Row, 1973.

Secondary Sources

Albert, Walter. "Yves Bonnefoy and the Architecture of Poetry." *Modern Language Notes* 82 (December 1967): 590-603.

Caws, Mary Ann. *The Inner Theatre of Recent French Poetry*. Princeton: Princeton University Press, 1972.

Gordon, Alex. "Things Dying, Things New Born: The Poetry of Yves Bonnefoy." *Mosaic* 6 (1973): 55-70.

Lawall, Sarah. "Yves Bonnefoy and Denis Roche: Art and the Art of Poetry." In *About French Poetry from Dada to Tel Quel: Text and Theory*, edited by M.A. Caws, pp. 69-95. Detroit: Wayne State University Press, 1974.

____, and Caws, Mary Ann. "A Style of Silence: Two Readings of Yves Bonnefoy's Poetry." *Contemporary Literature* 16 (Spring 1975): 193-217.

Maurin, Mario. "On Bonnefoy's Poetry." *Yale French Studies*, no. 21 (Spring-Summer 1958), pp. 16-22.

St. Aubyn, F. C. "Yves Bonnefoy: First Existentialist Poet." *Chicago Review* 17 (1964): 118-29.

DATE DUE
